CW00495124

SHORT WALKS ORKNEY ISLANDS

by Graham Uney

CICERONE

Walkers enjoying sea views at Yesnaby Castle (Walk 7)

CONTENTS

USING THIS GUIDE

Routes in this book

In this book you will find a selection of easy or moderate walks suitable for almost everyone, including casual walkers and families with children, or for when you only have a short time to fill. The routes have been carefully chosen to allow you to explore the area and its attractions. Most routes are circular or out-and-back, although some linear walks may be included that use public transport to get back to the start. Although there may be some climbs there is no challenging terrain, but do bear in mind that conditions can sometimes be wet or muddy underfoot. A route summary table is included on page 6 to help you choose the right walk.

Clothing and footwear

You won't need any special equipment to enjoy these walks. The weather in Britain can be changeable, so choose clothing suitable for the season and wear or carry a waterproof jacket. For footwear, comfortable walking boots or trainers with a good grip are best. A small rucksack for drinks, snacks and spare clothing is useful. See www.adventuresmart.uk.

Walk descriptions

At the beginning of each walk you'll find all the information you need:

- start/finish location, with postcode and a what3words address to help you find it
- parking and transport information, estimated walking time, total distance and climb
- details of public toilets available along the route and where you can get refreshments
- a summary of the key highlights of the walk and what you might see

Timings given are the time to complete the walk at a reasonable walking pace. Allow extra time for extended stops or if walking with children.

The route is described in clear, easy-to-follow directions, with each waypoint marked on an accompanying map extract. It's a good idea to read the whole of the route instructions before setting out, so that you know what to expect.

Maps, GPX files and what3words

Extracts from the OS® 1:25,000 map accompany each route. GPX files for all the walks in this book are available to download at www.cicerone.co.uk/1193/gpx.

What3words is a free smartphone app which identifies every 3m square of the globe with a unique three-word address, e.g. ///destiny.cafe.sonic. For more information see https://what3words.com/products/what3words-app.

Walking with children

Even young children can be surprisingly strong walkers, but every family is different and you may need to adapt the timings given in this book to take that into account. Make sure you go at the pace of the slowest member and choose a walk with an exciting objective in mind, such as a cave, river, waterfall or picnic spot. Many of the walks can be shortened to suit – suggestions are included at the end of the route description.

Dogs

Sheep or cattle may be found grazing on a number of these walks. Keep dogs under control at all times so that they don't scare or disturb livestock or wildlife. Cattle, particularly cows with calves, may occasionally pose a risk to walkers with dogs. If you ever feel threatened by cattle, let go of your dog's lead and let it run free. Always bag and bin dog poo, or take it home.

Enjoying the countryside responsibly

Enjoy the countryside and treat it with respect to protect our natural environments. In Scotland, you can enjoy the outdoors on most land and inland water, as long as you act responsibly and follow the Scottish Outdoor Access Code – www.outdooraccess-scotland.scot.

The Scottish Outdoor Access Code

Responsible access can be enjoyed over most of Scotland including parks, hills, moors, mountains and woods, beaches and the coast, lochs, rivers and canals, and some areas of farmland. The key principles are:

Take responsibility for your own actions

- park sensibly and do not create an obstruction
- take your rubbish home

Respect the interests of other people

- respect the needs of other people enjoying or working in the outdoors
- follow any reasonable advice from land managers
- on farmland, leave gates as you find them and keep to unsown ground, field edges or paths
- access rights do not usually apply to farmyards, but if a well-used path goes through a farmyard, you can follow it
- paths are shared with others – let people know you are coming so you do not alarm them, and slow down, stop or stand aside if needed

Care for the environment

- don't disturb or damage wildlife or historic places
- never light open fires, barbecues or fire bowls in dry periods or near to forests, farmland, buildings or historic sites at any time
- never cut down or damage trees

ROUTE SUMMARY TABLE

WALK NAME	START POINT	TIME	DISTANCE
1. Kirkwall town trail and the Peerie Sea	The Orkney Distillery and Visitor Centre, Kirkwall	2hr	4km (2½ miles)
2. Wideford Hill and chambered cairn	Pickaquoy Leisure Centre, Kirkwall	3hr	9.5km (6 miles)
3. Skara Brae and Bay of Skaill	Skara Brae Visitor Centre	3hr	4km (2½ miles)
4. Brough of Deerness and Mull Head	Mull Head car park near Deerness	3hr	6km (3¾ miles)
5. Marwick Head	Marwick Bay	3hr	4.5km (2¾ miles)
6. Brough of Birsay and the Earl's Palace	Point of Buckquoy near Birsay	3hr	6km (3¾ miles)
7. Yesnaby Castle and the Brough of Bigging	Yesnaby clifftop	2hr	4km (2½ miles)
8. Stromness and the Sands of Warebeth	Stromness Northlink Ferry Terminal	3hr	7km (4¼ miles)
9. Hoy: The Old Man of Hoy	Rackwick Hostel	4hr	8.5km (5¼ miles)
10. Graemsay: Island circuit	Graemsay Ferry Terminal	3hr	10.5km (6½ miles)
11. Rousay: Mid Howe Cairn and Broch	Mid Howe Cairn car park	2hr	5km (3 miles)
12. Rousay: Faraclett Head	Faraclett near Banks	2hr	3.5km (2¼ miles)
13. Eday: Ward Hill	Eday Ferry Terminal	3hr	9km (5½ miles)
14. Westray: Noup Head	Backarass near Pierowall	3hr	7km (4¼ miles)
15. Stronsay: The Vat of Kirbuster	Kirbuster	2hr	5.5km (3½ miles)

HIGHLIGHTS
Historic town, ancient earth house, lake and harbour views
Hilltop views and an ancient burial chamber
Neolithic village site and beach walk
Spectacular clifftop views and a blow hole
Seabird colonies on huge sea cliffs
Historic island across a tidal causeway
Spectacular clifftop views and a sea stack
Historic town and a beautiful beach
Maritime heath and iconic sea stack
Away-from-it-all walk on a quiet island
Ancient broch and cairn, and a coastal walk
Moorland walk to coastal headland
Highest point of a lovely island
Seabird cliffs on a remote island
Wild cliffs on a remote and beautiful island

SYMBOLS USED ON ROUTE MAPS

S	Start point
F	Finish point
SF	Start and finish at the same place
4 →	Waypoint
~	Route line

MAPPING IS SHOWN AT A SCALE OF 1:25,000

0 KM — 0.25 — 0.5
0 miles — 0.25

DOWNLOAD THE GPX FILES FOR FREE AT
www.cicerone.co.uk/1193/GPX

Marwick Head and the Kitchener Memorial (Walk 5)

INTRODUCTION

A group of walkers at Yesnaby (Walk 7)

The Orkney Islands are a magical place to visit. For many people coming to these beautiful islands the chief appeal is the extraordinary number of internationally important Neolithic archaeological sites, while others visit Orkney for the many poignant reminders of our wartime history, or to rediscover their own Viking heritage. Some come for close-up views of some of the UK's most charismatic and impressive wildlife species, or just to relax in the clean air and take in the stunning scenery that abounds throughout these islands.

Walking on the Orkney Islands

The walking on the Orkney Islands tends to take you either along coastal cliffs or sandy beaches, or to the top of the hills, which are small, but give commanding views of the islands all around. For many of these walks the terrain is rough grassland or stony clifftops, and sometimes pathless. Finding your way is usually easy, though, as often you just have to keep the sea to your left or right! Some, but not all walks are signposted, and all are circular or out and back routes.

One thing you can be sure about, on Orkney you're never very far away from the sea. You'll see spectacular arches and pinnacles of rock known as stacks, and the coastline is indented with deep rocky inlets known locally as 'geos'. Every island has its own unique character and scenery. On the main island, known here simply as Mainland, you can find yourself enjoying town trails, coastal cliff and beach walks, hill walks, and traditional crofting farmland. The islands of Graemsay, Hoy, Rousay, Eday, Westray and Stronsay, all of which are featured in this book, are well worth discovering too, and you'll find yourself planning to revisit each of them.

In this guidebook there are eight walks on Mainland, two on the islands to the south of Mainland, Hoy and Graemsay, then five on the north islands of Rousay, Eday, Westray, and Stronsay. All the walks on the islands are reached via ferries, and some need further transport once you are on the island. Where taxis or hire bikes are available, or if it would be better to take your own vehicle over on the ferry, this is suggested in the introduction for each walk.

Special things to see

Most visitors will want to spend time enjoying the delights of the old towns of both Kirkwall and Stromness. There are plenty of historic buildings, and you may want to spend at least a full day in each town.

Right at the top of your list of things to see should be the UNESCO 'Heart of Neolithic Orkney' World Heritage Site. The four archaeological sites that make up the Heart of Orkney – Skara Brae, Ring of Brodgar, Stones of Stennes, and Maeshowe – are the most important Neolithic remains in Western Europe, although there are many lesser-known archaeological sites of local importance too.

Equally important, and of more recent historical significance, are the many wartime reminders and monuments around Orkney. These include the Churchill Barriers around Scapa

The Ring of Brodgar, one of the most impressive Neolithic monuments on Orkney

A walker enjoying the spectacle of one of Orkney's biggest sea cliffs (Walk 5)

Flow, the Italian Chapel on Lamb Holm, and the Kitchener Memorial on Marwick Head. Going back further in time, the Covenanters Memorial on Deerness commemorates prisoners shipped to the American colonies in 1679.

Bases and places to stay

Kirkwall is the capital of the Orkney Islands and has a wide range of accommodation options. Most of the islands to the north of Mainland are accessed from Kirkwall, including Westray, Eday, and Stronsay, so if you are staying there you can visit a range of island walks just by jumping onto a ferry.

Stromness also has good accommodation options and is the point where you will catch a ferry to the islands of Hoy and Graemsay.

Getting there and around

Kirkwall airport is serviced by direct flights from Edinburgh, Glasgow, Aberdeen, and Inverness, and it is easy to get into Kirkwall itself from the airport via bus or taxi. Ferries to Orkney operate from Aberdeen to Kirkwall, linking onwards to Shetland if you want to visit there as well. Other ferries go from Scrabster, near Thurso, to Stromness, and from Gill's Bay to St Margaret's Hope.

Once on the islands, there is a reasonable bus service around Mainland, but for travel on the smaller islands a car or bike can be useful. It is possible to hire cars in Kirkwall if arriving by air.

For inter-island travel within Orkney, the Orkney Islands Council operate regular relatively inexpensive ferries to all the major islands.

Old houses down Bridge Street, Kirkwall

WALK 1

Kirkwall town trail and the Peerie Sea

Time 2hr
Distance 4km (2½ miles)
Climb 35m

Explore the old harbour town of Kirkwall, the capital of Orkney

Start/finish	*The Orkney Distillery and Visitor Centre, Kirkwall*
Locate	*KW15 1QX ///tested.resides.cherished*
Cafes/pubs	*Lots of options in Kirkwall*
Transport	*Buses from around Mainland go to Kirkwall*
Parking	*Waterfront West car park*
Toilets	*On Shapinsay Pier, opposite the start*

This short, easy walk around Kirkwall takes you from the bustling harbourside through the historic old town to St Magnus Cathedral, and the Bishop's and Earl's Palaces. Look for wildlife on the Peerie Sea, a unique lake in the centre of town, then visit the nearby Iron Age Grain Earth House (pick up the key from the Judith Glue shop during the walk if you want to go inside).

Kirkwall harbour

1 Facing across the road to the sea, start by crossing the road, then walking right. There are views of the busy harbour on your left, with ferries and fishing boats coming and going. Keep on beyond the first roundabout until you come to the Orkney Ferries building on your left. Cross the road to Bridge Street. Walk down Bridge Street, turning right at its end onto Albert Street. Look for the Big Tree on the right and carry on to the junction with Broad Street.

The Big Tree on Albert Street

The Big Tree was named 'Scotland's Tree of the Year 2017' in a competition organised by the Woodland Trust. It was planted by Thomas Sclater in the 1870s, along with two others, in what was then his garden.

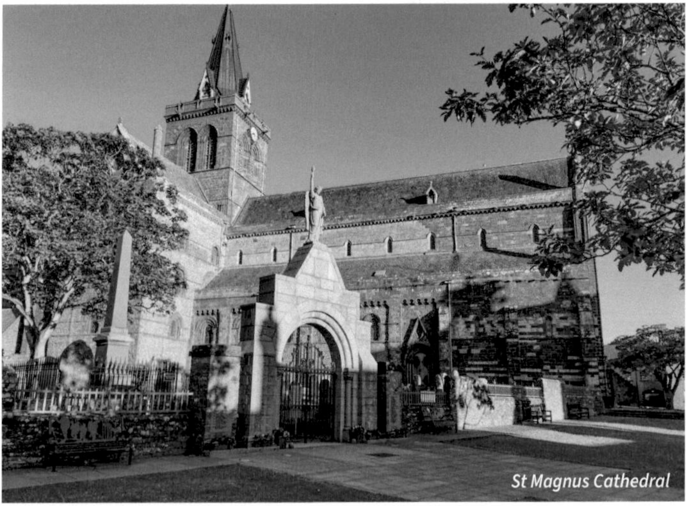
St Magnus Cathedral

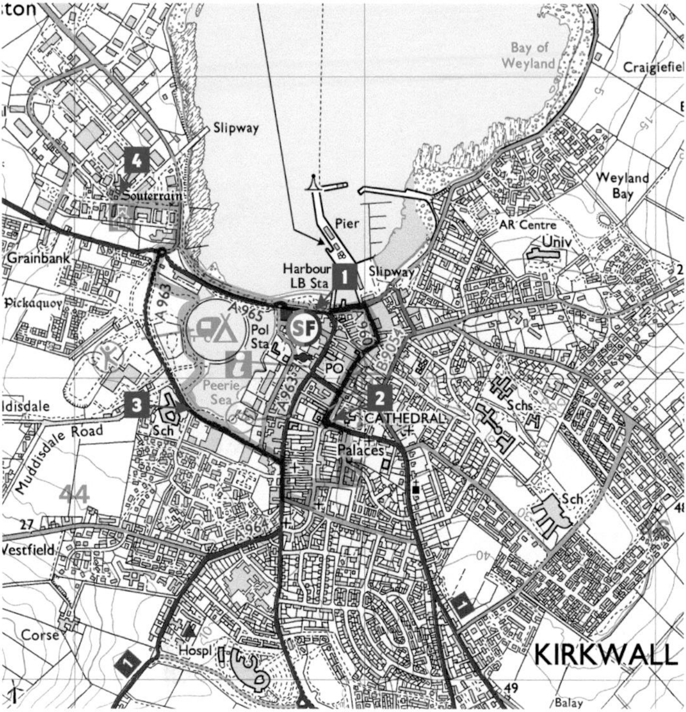

Continue onto Broad Street with **St Magnus Cathedral** on your left. Building started on the cathedral in 1137. It is the most northerly cathedral in the UK, and the oldest in Scotland. Opposite the cathedral is the Judith Glue Shop and Real Food Cafe. Go in there and ask for the key for the Grain Earth House visited later in this walk.

2 With the cathedral to your left follow the path round into Palace Road. Within 100m look for the **Bishop's and Earl's Palaces** on the right.

The Bishop's Palace dates back to the 12th century when Kirkwall was a thriving Norwegian port. It was part of the cathedral complex. The Earl's Palace was built in the 1600s by Patrick Stewart, the Earl of Orkney.

The grassy mound of the Grain Earth House

Turn right and walk down Watergate to its end at a T-junction. Turn right onto Victoria Road. Turn left at the T-junction onto Victoria Street, then right onto Union Street. Go right on Junction Road and left at the round-about onto Pickaquoy Road. Follow this until you can see the **Peerie Sea**, a large man-made lake, on the right.

When the town was built a spit of land known as The Ayre was created to help reclaim the marsh-land, and the Peerie Sea is part of this. Today it is an important place for overwintering ducks and waders.

3 Cross to the footpath alongside the Peerie Sea and walk clockwise around it until you come to the circular Model Yacht Lake. Follow the path, keeping the lake to your right, until you come to a path leading across a playing field back to Pickaquoy Road. Turn right and walk to the roundabout. Walk straight ahead here along Grainshore Road, then turn second left up through the Scott's Road industrial estate. After 200m look for Swordfish Road on the right, and you'll see the grassy mound of the Grain Earth House immediately on your right. If you collected the key from Judith Glue's shop you can

ⓘ The name Orkney comes from the Old Norse name Orkneyjar (pronounced ork-nee-yar) which means 'seal islands'.

climb down into the chamber of this Iron Age earth house.

4 Retrace your steps along Scott's Road to return to Grainshore Road. Just before the roundabout at Pickaquoy Road turn left to walk along the shore back to the Orkney Distillery.

– To shorten

Head back to the harbour easily from any point on the walk.

+ To lengthen

Combine with Walk 2 to climb Wideford Hill by crossing Pickaquoy Road after leaving the Peerie Sea and heading towards the obvious Leisure Centre where Walk 2 starts. You can then visit the Grain Earth House at the end of the combined walks.

Kirkwall as a Norwegian Port

Orkney was annexed by the Kingdom of Norway and settled by the Norsemen from around the year AD875. In 1472 Orkney was accepted by King James III of Scotland as a marriage dowry from the family of his bride, Margaret of Denmark, in lieu of payment of 50,000 florins. Christian I, the king of Denmark, was an impoverished ruler, and offering the Orkney Islands to Scotland would have been easier than finding that amount of money. Orkney became part of Scotland, and the Shetland Islands were handed over to Scotland in the same year, in lieu of a further payment of 8000 florins.

The Bishop's and Earl's Palaces

The path on Wideford Hill

WALK 2

Wideford Hill and chambered cairn

Time 3hr
Distance 9.5km (6 miles)
Climb 330m

Commanding views over Kirkwall and an ancient burial chamber

Start/finish	*Pickaquoy Leisure Centre, Kirkwall*
Locate	*KW15 1LR ///regret.looms.aquatics*
Cafes/pubs	*Small coffee shop in the leisure centre*
Transport	*Buses from around Mainland go to Kirkwall*
Parking	*Muddisdale Road car park*
Toilets	*In leisure centre next to the car park*

Wideford Hill is one of the most prominent hills in Mainland Orkney. With a little uphill effort you can enjoy expansive views from the top across the whole of Kirkwall, the rest of Mainland, and across Wide Firth to the islands of Shapinsay, Eday, and Stronsay. On the way to the summit you can visit the Wideford Hill Cairn and climb down into the depths of the tomb.

The Wideford Hill Cairn

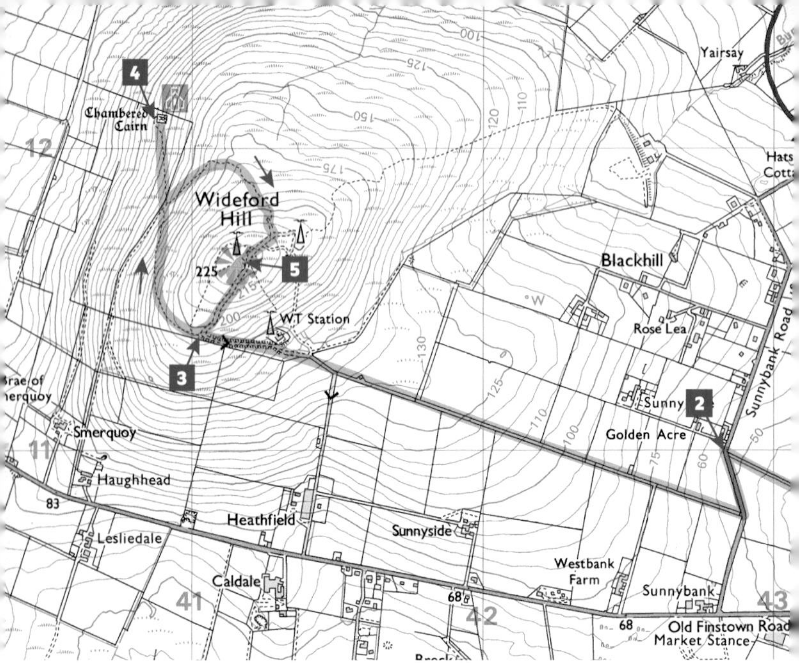

1 From the main door of the leisure centre walk along the exit road and turn right down **Muddisdale Road**. Turn right and continue along Muddisdale Road, keeping a new housing development to your left. Where the road swings to the left at the houses, go straight on along a track.

> ⓘ *Of Orkney's 70 islands, 20 are inhabited, with the main islands being Mainland, Hoy, Rousay, Westray, North Ronaldsay, Shapinsay, Eday, Sanday, Stronsay, Burray, and South Ronaldsay.*

Pass Muddisdale Farm then the golf course, both on your right, and come out onto **Sunnybank Road**.

2 Turn left along the road and in just over 100m turn right onto a track on a bend. This track goes in a straight line uphill and emerges onto a narrow lane on the upper slopes of Wideford Hill. Follow the lane uphill to where it bends sharply to the right by a little car park on the left with an interpretation board.

3 At the bend leave the road and go left on a good path that skirts around the heathery hillside, then descends

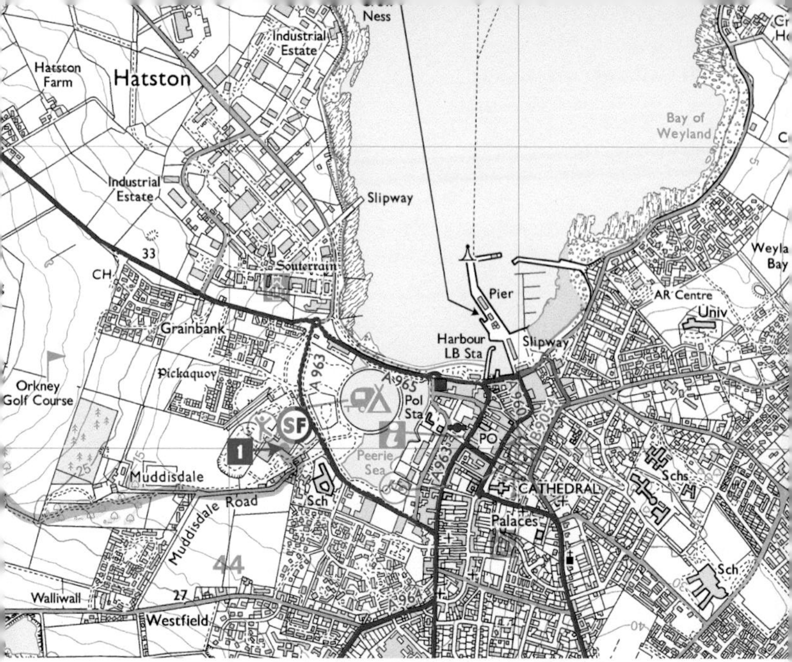

Walkers leaving the cairn to head towards Wideford Hill

The path leading back down the hill to Kirkwall

to a gate through a fence. Ignore the path to your right for now – you'll go that way once you have visited the chambered cairn. Go through the gate and continue along the path to reach the **Wideford Hill Cairn**. There is a gate into the enclosure, and on a post on the left as you go up to the cairn you'll see a box. Take the torch out of the box and go to the top of the cairn to slide back the metal lid. Now climb down the steep ladder into the tomb!

The Wideford Hill Cairn is a burial chamber dating back 5000 years. Its position in a prominent place overlooking the whole of the west side of Mainland and the islands to the north is probably significant, although we do not know who was buried here.

4 Once you've finished in the tomb, turn off the torch and put it back in the box. Now retrace your steps to the gate through the fence. Just beyond the fence take the path off to the left that you spotted earlier. This goes uphill, steeply at first then more gently as it curves around the side of Wideford Hill. Just beyond a boggy section the path emerges onto a tarmac road. Turn right and climb to the summit of **Wideford Hill** with a concrete trig point, and lots of masts and aerials.

5 From the summit, after taking in the views, go down the road to the bend. Turn left down the road you walked on earlier, and make sure to turn left again where the road bends sharply downhill to the right. You should be on the long straight track that you walked up along. Retrace your steps back to the leisure centre.

– To shorten

Miss out the visit to the Wideford Hill Cairn by turning right at the interpretation board and going straight to the summit of Wideford Hill. This will cut 2km (45min) from the walk.

+ To lengthen

Combine with Walk 1.

Scapa Flow

From the summit of Wideford Hill look south across the expanse of Scapa Flow. This is an important place in our war-time history. During World War 1 a German U-boat was spotted in this huge natural harbour and British merchant ships were anchored here and deliberately sunk to block all the possible entrances into the strategic seaway. In World War 2 Churchill Barriers mainly made of concrete blocks were constructed, and are now causeways linking the southern islands to Mainland. Towards the end of the war 74 German ships were interned in Scapa Flow, and they became something of a tourist attraction. Eventually, after 10 months, when the German Officer in Command realised that the end of the war was coming, he ordered that all the ships in his command be scuttled. Many were sunk in Scapa Flow and others were beached nearby. Most were later salvaged, but eight still remain.

Enjoying the solitude at Bay of Skaill

WALK 3

Skara Brae and the Bay of Skaill

Time 3hr
Distance 4km (2½ miles)
Climb 30m

An easy exploration of a unique Neolithic village, followed by a scenic walk along a lovely white-sand beach

Start/finish	*Skara Brae Visitor Centre*
Locate	*KW16 3LR ///readjust.blitz.pigtails*
Cafes/pubs	*Cafe in the visitor centre*
Transport	*Buses from Kirkwall and Stromness*
Parking	*Visitor Centre car park*
Toilets	*Toilets at the visitor centre (entry fee) and public toilets halfway around the bay*

For many visitors Skara Brae (entrance fee applies) is the main reason they come to Orkney. It is the best-preserved Neolithic site in Western Europe, and part of the UNESCO 'Heart of Neolithic Orkney' World Heritage Site. Visit Skara Brae and Skaill House with one single entrance ticket, then enjoy a short but exhilarating walk along the fabulous beach to the remains of a broch (fortified house) on the northern headland.

Skara Brae

Inside one of the houses at Skara Brae

1 From the car park you'll need to go through the visitor centre to buy an entrance ticket. There is a useful video to watch, lots of information and displays, and a recreation of what these Neolithic village sites probably looked like. From the recreated house follow the path along the 'Timeline' to where a gateway leads into **Skara Brae** Neolithic village. From a fixed walkway you can peer down into the exposed houses, and there are interpretation boards and informative staff on hand to answer your questions.

2 When you've spent some time at Skara Brae head back to the gate. There's a path from here on the right that leads to **Skaill House**.

Skaill House is a 17th-century manor house that has large collections of interesting things on display, including the dinner service from Captain Cook's ship, HMS *Resolution*.

3 Return to the visitor centre and go back out of the back door, but instead of heading to Skara Brae, once you're by the coast go down onto the beach and turn right, with the sea to your left. Walk along the beach, marvelling at the beautiful white sand, the views out to sea, and how quiet the beach is! At the far end, where the shore becomes rocky, go up onto the top of the low cliffs and follow them around to the **Knowe of Verron Broch**. This is the remains of an Iron Age fortified house.

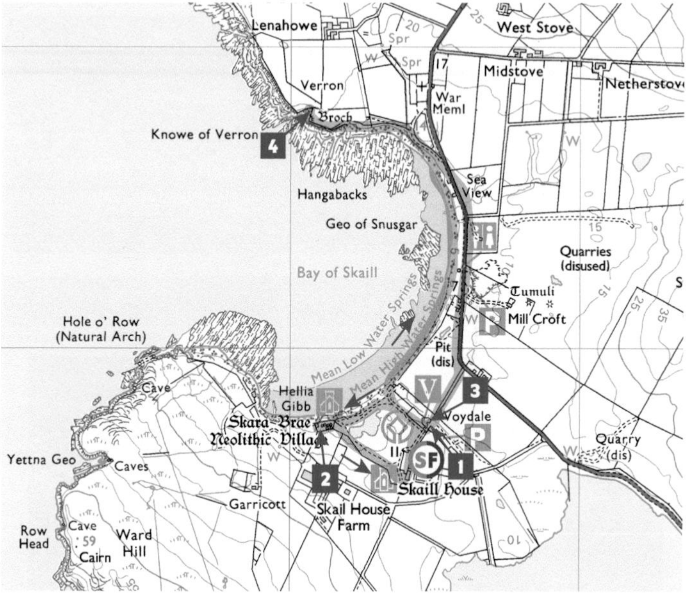

4 Retrace your steps for 500m, but instead of walking back along the beach follow the road back to the visitor centre. It's a fairly quiet lane and it has a public toilet block about halfway along if needed. You can return along the beach if you prefer.

The beautiful Bay of Skaill

– To shorten

Visit Skara Brae and Skaill House without doing the beach walk.

+ To lengthen

From Skara Brae it is possible to go west along the shore for 1km to Hole o' Row, which is a natural arch, but the going is rough underfoot. Allow an extra 1hr for the 2km return walk.

Skara Brae

Inside a reconstruction of a Neolithic house

Skara Brae is a 5000-year-old village site that was preserved by being buried under a sand dune. It is unique in that the stone furniture, fireplaces, drains, and even the damp-proof course can all be seen today. The village was lived in for around 600 years, but we don't know why the people left. In 1850 a violent storm raged across the north of Scotland and the sand that covered the hidden Skara Brae was blown away, giving modern humans the first inclination that there was something important buried there.

WALK 4

Brough of Deerness and Mull Head

Start/finish	*Mull Head car park at the end of the public road beyond Deerness village*
Locate	*KW17 2QJ ///inhales.tramps.printout*
Cafes/pubs	*None on route*
Transport	*Bus no. 3 to Deerness village (stops 2km from the start of the walk)*
Parking	*Mull Head car park*
Toilets	*At nearby visitor centre (free entry)*

Time 3hr
Distance 6km (3¾ miles)
Climb 140m

Spectacular clifftop walking with amazing views and an optional scramble to a rocky bluff

The walk round Deerness and Mull Head is one of the best in the Orkney Islands for sea views from clifftops. The Brough of Deerness is a rocky bluff that is almost detached from the Mainland. To reach it requires a steep walk down a path to the beach, and a rocky scramble protected by a fixed metal chain to ascend, but this can easily be omitted if you prefer.

Amazing views from the cliffs at Deerness

Looking out for wildlife at Deerness

1 From the right-hand corner of the car park, walk down a path that leads easily to a blowhole in the clifftop known as **The Gloup** because of the sound the waves make when pushed through on a rising tide or in a storm.

The Gloup would have been a cave initially, as the water action from the sea carved deep into the land along weaknesses and fissures. Eventually the cave roof collapsed, creating this blowhole.

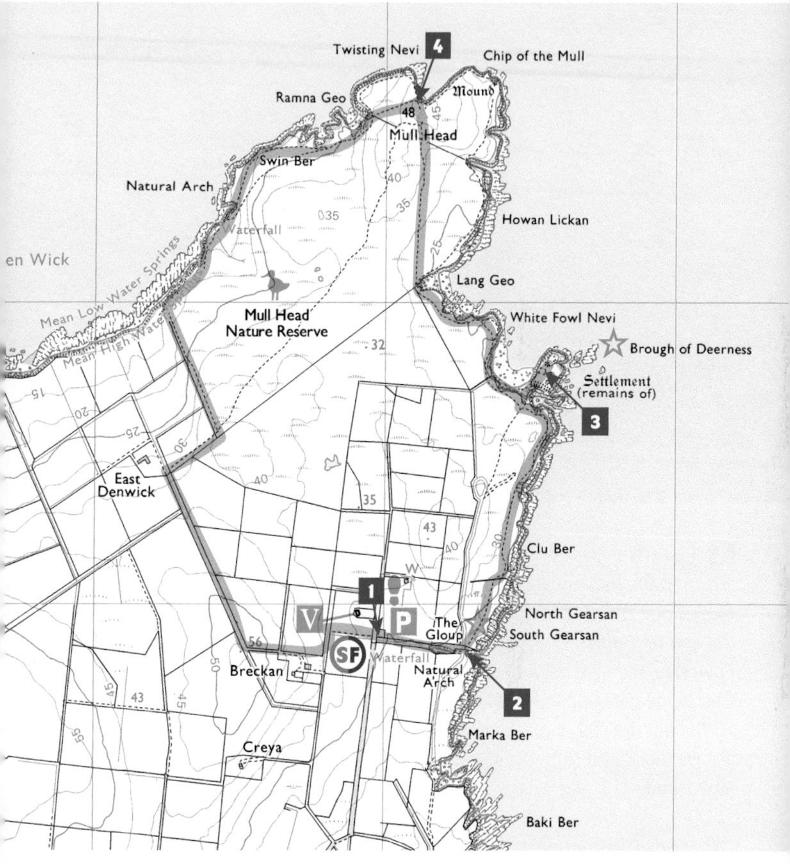

2 From The Gloup turn left along the clifftop path. Pass **Clu Ber** and continue to where you get a view of the **Brough of Deerness**. You can scramble out onto the Brough if you wish. A steep path leads down to the notch between the land and the Brough, and a rough scramble on rock protected by a fixed chain leads up the other side. There are the remains of a Viking Age settlement on top of the Brough of Deerness, but there's not a huge amount left to see today.

The chain-protected path up onto the Brough of Deerness

3 From the Brough of Deerness return to the main headland and turn right along the clifftop path, keeping the sea to your right. Go past **White Fowl Nevi** then the bay known as Lang Geo before coming to a kissing gate. From here the easy path goes directly across moorland to the trig point on **Mull Head**.

Mull Head was designated as a Local Nature Reserve in 1963, in recognition of its importance for wildlife, geology, and history. It's a good example of maritime heathland, and hosts small numbers of seabirds on its cliffs, including fulmars, shags, and black guillemots.

4 Turn left and follow the path, again along the clifftop, with great views across Deer Sound to Rerwick Head. At a boardwalk turn left, with a fence to your right. The clifftop path continues to the Covenanters Memorial, visible ahead. If not visiting the memorial head uphill away from the coast. Turn right at a kissing gate near the top of the hill, then left onto a track. Go left at a small wind turbine, then left again just past the croft at **Breckan**. The next right turn leads you back to the car park.

ⓘ *Orkney's biggest landowner is nature conservation charity the RSPB, which owns 113 nature reserves here.*

− To shorten

Walk as far as the Brough of Deerness, then return. This would reduce the distance to 2km (about 1hr).

+ To lengthen

On the return along the clifftop, where you come to the boardwalk, continue along the coast to visit the Covenanters Memorial. This adds a further 3km, returning to the boardwalk to finish the walk. Allow 1hr more.

The Covenanters Memorial

The Covenanters Memorial commemorates 257 Covenanter prisoners who were to be shipped to the American colonies as servants in 1679. (Covenanters were Scottish Presbyterians who signed the National Covenant in 1683 in opposition to the Stuart kings). On 10 December 1679 a storm wrecked the ship on the rocks here. The captain and crew had locked most of the prisoners below deck, and only 50 men survived.

The path beside the farm at Breckan

Marwick Head – a seabird city

WALK 5

Marwick Head

Start/finish	*Marwick Bay*
Locate	*KW17 2NB ///clown.dummy.estimated*
Cafes/pubs	*None on route*
Transport	*Bus no. 8 to the main road junction (1.5km from the start of the walk)*
Parking	*Car park at Marwick Bay*
Toilets	*No public toilets on route*

Time 2hr
Distance 4.5km (2¾ miles)
Climb 150m

Walk on good paths along the huge cliffs at Marwick Head, one of the best places on Orkney to see thousands of nesting seabirds

A truly magnificent walk along the clifftop path at Marwick Head. This RSPB Nature Reserve is an important seabird colony, and one of the best places on Orkney to see puffins, guillemots, razorbills, and a whole host of other seabirds. The scenery is spectacular at any time of year, and you get to visit the Kitchener Memorial too. It's an easy walk after the first short uphill section, on good paths throughout, but the clifftop is unfenced, so care is needed.

Looking for puffins at Marwick Head

1 Walk back along the track with the shore to your left, continuing beyond the road you drove in on, until you reach the end of the beach at **The Choin**. This massive low-tide lagoon lies between the beach and the open sea. The name comes from the Old Norse word *tjörn* which means 'large pool'. The path goes left at a junction and leads uphill, with the coastal cliffs below to your left. Above the rocky platform of **Choldertoo** the cliffs start to get very high, and care is needed. The path goes close to the edge as you approach a fence.

2 Cross the fence and continue to the **Kitchener Memorial** set atop the highest point on the cliffs.

The Kitchener Memorial commemorates the crew of the HMS *Hampshire*, which was sunk here by a German mine in 1916. Lord Kitchener was one of the 700 people who lost their lives. There were only 12 survivors.

Continue along the clifftop, stopping to peer carefully down at the seabird colonies below. A short way beyond the memorial you'll see a path leading off to the right. Ignore this for now and go a little further along the cliffs to where you get a really good view back to the cliffs and seabird colonies on Marwick Head. There is a rock platform from which you can get a safe view of the full height of the cliffs.

The Kitchener Memorial on top of the cliffs at Marwick Head

Looking back along the cliffs towards the Kitchener Memorial

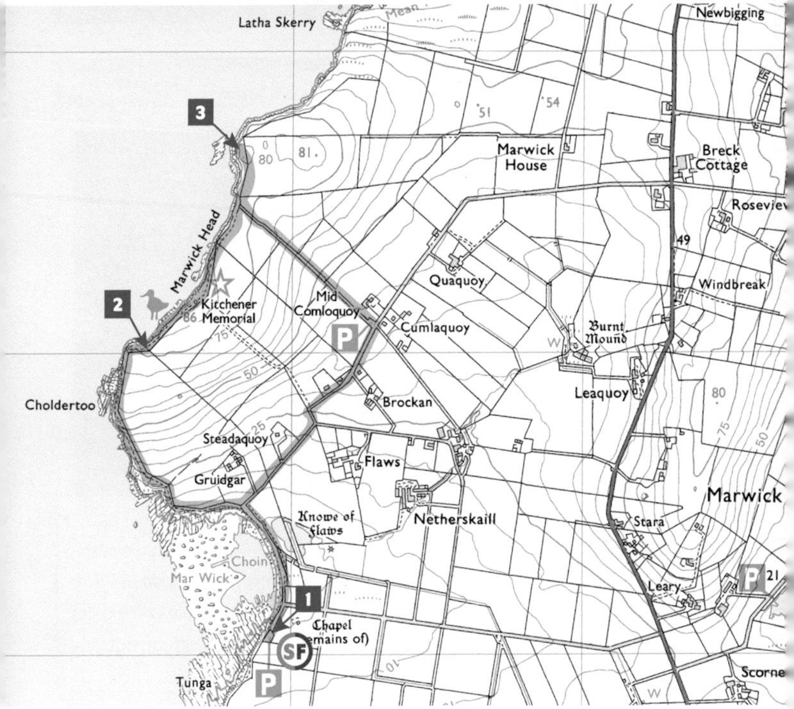

3 Return along the clifftop to the path junction, turn inland and follow the grassy track down to the road and a car park at **Cumlaquoy**. Turn right along the road. Go left around a sharp bend, then take the next right which leads back to the shore at Choin. Turn left here to return to the start.

– To shorten

Park at Cumlaquoy and head out to the Kitchener Memorial from there. This gives a walk of 2km (1hr).

+ To lengthen

Continue along the clifftop going north-east to Latha Skerry for views towards Birsay. This adds 2km (1hr) and involves a climb back uphill.

Marwick Head RSPB Reserve

Puffin at Marwick Head

Marwick Head is best visited for its seabird colonies from May through to the end of July. There are good nesting populations of guillemots, razorbills, kittiwakes, fulmars, and shags, and the numbers of breeding puffins is increasing. For that reason it is a Site of Special Scientific Interest and a Special Protection Area. The rocky beach at The Choin is a good place to see wading birds in winter, including purple sandpipers, turnstones, and ringed plovers. From Marwick Head you can also watch for dolphins and whales on a calm day, and you may see the rare great yellow bumblebee on the clifftop flowers.

WALK 6

Brough of Birsay and the Earl's Palace

Time 3hr
Distance 6km (3¾ miles)
Climb 100m

Walk across a causeway at low tide to an important historical island, then visit the Earl's Palace on your return

Start/finish	*Point of Buckquoy at the road end near Birsay*
Locate	*KW17 2LX ///feels.glorified.latitudes*
Cafes/pubs	*Tearoom near Earl's Palace*
Transport	*Bus no. 7 from Kirkwall and Stromness*
Parking	*Brough of Birsay car park*
Toilets	*Near the Earl's Palace (150m south along the road)*
Note	*The causeway is only accessible at low tide. Check local tide times by calling the Skara Brae Visitor Centre on 01856 841815*

This is an exciting walk across a causeway to an island that is the site of Pictish, Norse, and medieval remains. There are clifftop views from the lighthouse and the whole island is covered with wildflowers that thrive on the sandy soil, a wonderful habitat type known as machair. Back on Mainland, the return route visits the Earl's Palace via a quiet coastal walk.

The causeway out to the Brough of Birsay

The Brough of Birsay

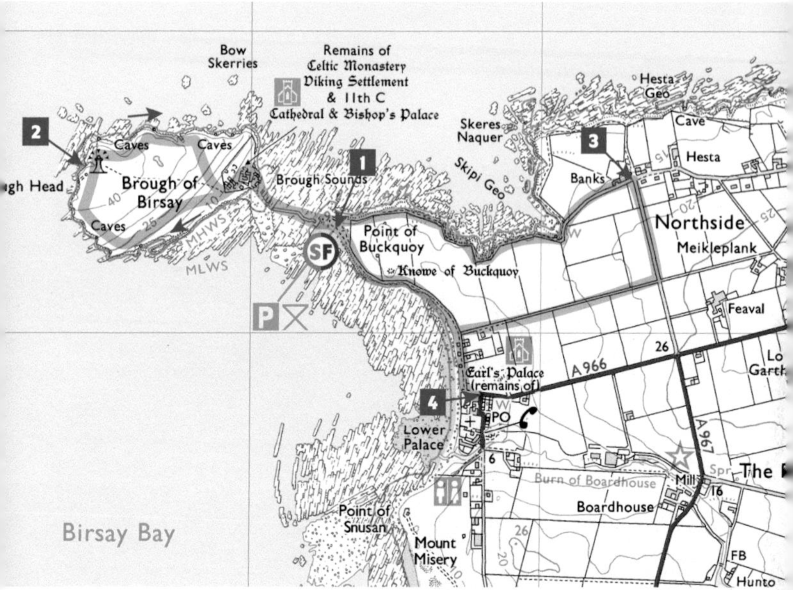

1 Having first checked the tide times (making sure it will be low tide during your visit), go down onto the causeway and walk between rockpools out to the **Brough of Birsay**. There is an admission charge, payable at the Historic Scotland booth upon entry.

Archaeological remains found on the island suggest that the Brough of Birsay was an important Pictish settlement. The Norse settled here in the 9th century, and there are the remains of a medieval church and monastery.

ⓘ Orkney has been inhabited for at least 8500 years, with archaeological remains dating back to Mesolithic times.

After you've looked around the Historic Scotland site, go out of the back gate and head for the coast. Walk anticlockwise around the island to the lighthouse. The lighthouse was built in 1925 by David Alan Stevenson, cousin of the author Robert Louis Stevenson.

The lighthouse at the Brough of Birsay

2 Continue anticlockwise around the island, back through the Historic Scotland site, then back across the causeway. As you reach the car park take the path on the left side of the headland. Follow this above the low cliffs to the rocky cleft of **Skipi Geo**. As the path turns around the back of the bay, look for a track on the right that goes inland to the hamlet of **Banks**.

ⓘ People from Orkney are called Orcadians, and don't really like being referred to as 'Scottish'. This relates to their strong Viking heritage.

3 At Banks turn right along the road. Within 400m turn right again along a track and follow this to the road that leads to the car park. Turn left at the road junction, then left again to reach the ruins of the **Earl's Palace**. This is well worth a visit to understand the role of the Orkney Earls.

4 Return to the road, turn right and walk back along it to the car park at **Brough of Birsay**.

The Earl's Palace

The Earl's Palace at Birsay

The Earl's Palace at Birsay was built between 1569 and 1574, and was the residence of Robert Stewart, the illegitimate son of James V and his mistress Euphemia Elphinstone. Robert Stewart was half-brother to Mary Queen of Scots. He was a tyrant, and his son Patrick Stewart – known as Black Patie because of his murderous ways – succeeded him. Black Patie was arrested in 1609 and condemned to death, but his execution had to be delayed until he had learned to recite the Lord's Prayer.

– To shorten

This walk can be done as two separate loops: one around the Brough of Birsay of 2.5km (1hr), and the other out to Northside, returning via the Earl's Palace, of 4.5km (2hr).

+ To lengthen

From Skipi Geo you can continue around the next headland as far as the rocky cleft of Hesta Geo and take the track inland to Banks from there. This adds 500m (10min).

Yesnaby Castle viewed from the side

WALK 7

Yesnaby Castle and the Brough of Bigging

Time 2hr
Distance 4km (2½ miles)
Climb 100m

Big cliffs and big seas, plus the chance to find one of the UK's smallest and rarest wildflowers

Start/finish	*Clifftop car park at Yesnaby*
Locate	*KW16 3LP ///acclaimed.sweetener.predict*
Cafes/pubs	*None on route*
Transport	*No public transport*
Parking	*Car park at Yesnaby*
Toilets	*No public toilets on route*

Easy walking on grassy paths gives access to magnificent coastal scenery, with caves, geos, sea stacks, and massive cliffs. The clifftops are unfenced, so care is required. Yesnaby is one of the few places where you can see the tiny Scottish primrose, if you can spot it, and there are a host of other interesting maritime heath plants to discover on this walk.

The Brough of Bigging

1 From the parking area walk along the clifftop with the sea to your right, passing the remains of wartime buildings. This was a World War 2 anti-aircraft battery manned by the Royal Navy to protect the western approaches to Scapa Flow. Within 400m of the car park the path starts to converge with the fence to your left. Here, between the path and the fence, is the best place to look for the tiny Scottish primrose. The path takes you downhill to a stream crossing at the back of the bay known as the **Noust of Bigging**.

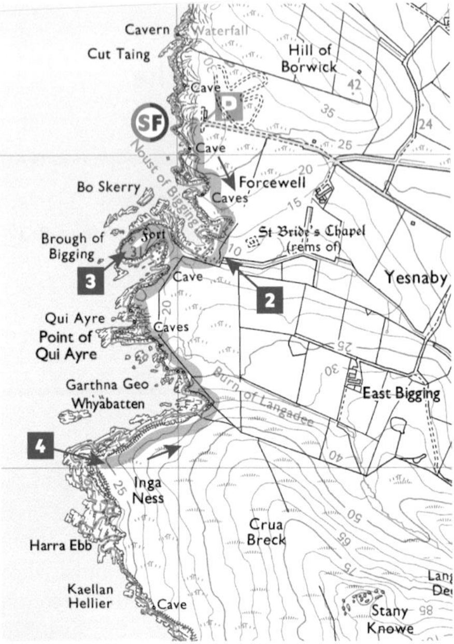

The Scottish Primrose, Primula scotica

The Scottish primrose, *Primula scotica*, can be seen between May and July. It is classed as 'nationally scarce' and is endemic to the north of Scotland in Orkney, Caithness, and Sutherland, meaning it can't be found anywhere else in the world.

2 Cross the little stream via a footbridge, then follow the path to the right, going slightly uphill and keeping the coastal cliffs to your right as you climb to the **Brough of Bigging**. The Brough of Bigging is the site of

Yesnaby Castle and the view back to the Brough of Bigging

a promontory fort dating back to around 1100BC. All that remains are three grass-covered banks.

3 Continue around the Brough of Bigging, following the coast around what is known as the Peedie Inlet.

At the entrance to the Peedie Inlet you'll see a pillar that is almost a sea stack. It's connected to the Mainland via a rock arch and is known to rock climbers as the False Stack, for obvious reasons!

Over the next small headland you get your first view of the Yesnaby Castle, which is not a castle at all but a sea stack. Continue around the broad bay of **Garthna Geo**. This can be a good place to spot seals basking on rocks at low tide, or bobbing round when the seas are high. The path continues around the bay and over short-cropped grass to the headland of **Inga Ness**.

4 From here your route back is to retrace your steps around all the same headlands you came out by, or for a very slightly shorter return, when you reach the fence around Garthna Geo you can follow it back to the car park.

+ To lengthen

From Inga Ness you can carry on along the coast as far as you wish, remembering of course that you have to come back the same way.

A walker comes around the headland at the Sands of Warebeth

WALK 8

Stromness and the Sands of Warebeth

Start/finish	*Stromness Northlink Ferry Terminal*
Locate	*KW16 3BH ///chapels.inclines.billiard*
Cafes/pubs	*Lots of choice in Stromness*
Transport	*Ferry direct from Scrabster in Scotland. Buses from Kirkwall*
Parking	*Ferry Road East car park*
Toilets	*In car park*

Time 3hr
Distance 7km (4¼ miles)
Climb 90m

Explore the fishing town of Stromness and enjoy views of Hoy from the Sands of Warebeth

An easy walk out from the old town of Stromness, taking in the quiet backroads to reach the lovely beach at the Sands of Warebeth, then returning via the popular coastal path that leads to Ness Point before a stroll through the oldest part of Stromness. The walk is easy to follow throughout, and is partly on tarmac, with the coastal section being on a good path.

The lovely harbour town of Stromness

1 From the **Northlink Ferry Terminal**, cross the car park and the main road to find Miller's Close. Go up Miller's Close as far as the crossroads with John Street and turn left. Walk along John Street, which becomes Victoria Street, then take Boys Lane on the right just beyond Brown's Hostel. Walk uphill to the end of Boys Lane and turn left onto Franklin Road. Walk along Franklin Road to reach a crossroads, with Church Road to the left and Christie's Brae to the right. Go up Christie's Brae to Back Road, turn left and keep going until you reach a roundabout.

2 At the roundabout go straight ahead onto Outertown Road. Go straight ahead at the crossroads, and slightly uphill with a little valley to your left as you start to leave

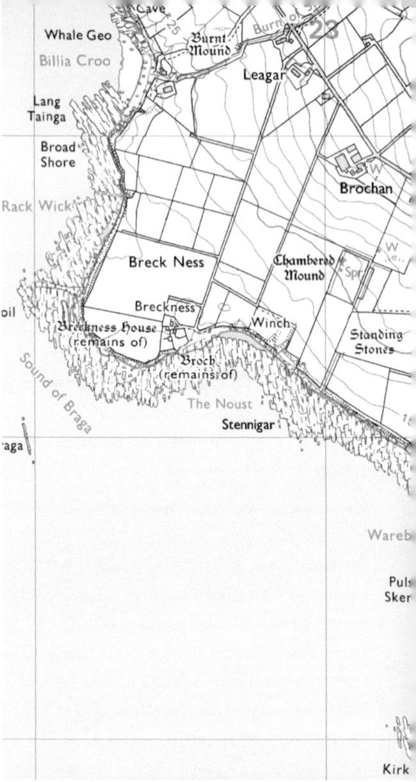

Sunlight on Hoy Sound as storm clouds clear over Hoy

the houses of Stromness behind. Take the second left at the top of the hill, marked as Warebeth Road. This little lane goes downhill, giving magnificent views across Hoy Sound to the hills of Hoy beyond. Carry on down Warebeth Road to reach the cemetery. Just as you get to the car park for the cemetery take the lane on the right and walk down to the beach at the **Sands of Warebeth**.

The Hoy Sound is a wild stretch of water and is the western entrance to Scapa Flow. Across the Sound is the island of Hoy, famous for its sea stack, the Old Man. Hoy is the hilliest of all the Orkney Islands.

A couple enjoying the walk towards Stromness

ⓘ *Orkney is closer to the Arctic Circle (524 miles) than it is to London (528 miles).*

3 Enjoy a stroll on Warebeth beach, then pick up the little path that runs along the grassy top of the beach, going in the direction of Hoy with the sea on your right. The path is a delight to walk, with expansive views across to Hoy and eventually to the island of Graemsay as you approach the headland. Ignore turnings to the left and just keep on the path to **Point of Ness**, with the sea to your right the whole way.

4 At Point of Ness turn left through the campsite and soon find yourself walking back into **Stromness**. Ness Road leads into South End, which at Stromness Museum becomes Albert Street. The museum is well worth a visit if you have time. Albert Street becomes Dundas Street, which leads between lots of interesting and picturesque old fishermen's houses back to the start.

+ To lengthen

Instead of turning down Warebeth Road, continue along Outertown Road as far as Leagar, then down a track to Breckness House. Walk back along the coast from Breckness, rejoining the main route at Waypoint 3. This is a much longer undertaking (adds 7km and 2hr).

The history of Stromness

The bay at Stromness is known as Hamnavoe (a name given to one of the ferries that comes into Stromness from Scrabster today). The earliest settlements date back to around the 16th century, and there was a seaman's inn here as far back as 1590. Between 1688 and 1815 conflict between Britain and France made passage through the English Channel difficult, and many ships came north around Scotland instead, often calling in at Stromness. The town grew quickly, and by 1702 the Canadian Hudson Bay Company had started recruiting men from Stromness. By the end of the 18th century three-quarters of the Hudson Bay Company workforce were Orcadian men.

In the old town of Stromness

The Old Man of Hoy

WALK 9

Hoy: The Old Man of Hoy

CHALLENGE ROUTE

Time 4hr
Distance 8.5km (5¼ miles)
Climb 600m

A real adventure on the island of Hoy, taking you across moorland to the famous sea stack, the Old Man of Hoy

Start/finish	*Rackwick Hostel*
Locate	*KW16 3NJ ///stuck.banquets.ambition*
Cafes/pubs	*Cafe at Moaness*
Transport	*Ferry (foot passengers only) from Stromness to Hoy (Moaness), then shared taxi to Rackwick (call Mr Clark on 01856 791315)*
Parking	*In Stromness at the Northlink Ferry Terminal*
Toilets	*In Stromness and at Moaness*

You'll need to allow a full day for this visit to Hoy. The spectacular walk out and back to the Old Man takes you into some relatively remote terrain, albeit on a good path. There are steep drops from the cliff edge, all of it unfenced, so care is needed. The final part from Stours Kinora is over pathless terrain with no waymarkers, but you can just retrace your steps instead if you wish. On the return ask the taxi driver to let you jump out halfway to look at the Dwarfie Stone.

Walkers high above Rackwick Bay

1 From the Rackwick Hostel walk along the path to a little wooded gorge. Turn right and go up through the gorge, then left to the Cra'as Nest. This is a small open museum dedicated to island life and crofting. It's easy to miss, so look for the grass-roofed croft houses as you go. Beyond the Cra'as Nest the path climbs diagonally across the flank of **Moor Fea Hill**. You'll soon find yourself above the big broken cliffs of **Too of the Head**.

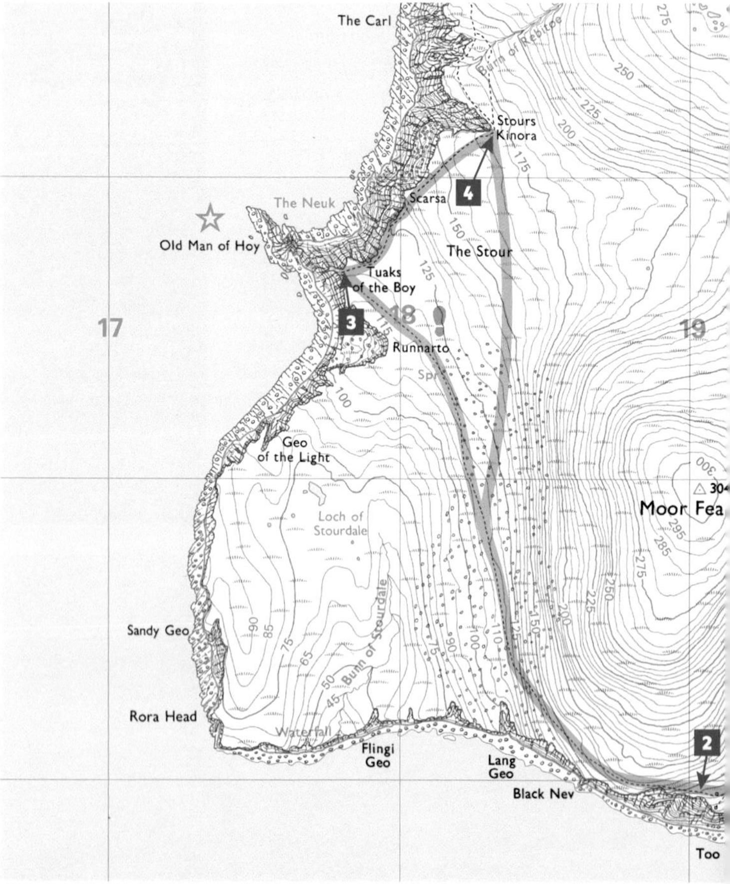

The Cra'as Nest Museum at Rackwick

2 Beyond this the path swings away from the sea cliffs and north through bouldery moorland. Keep going on the path, looking out for nesting great and Arctic skuas (known as bonxies and skootie alans locally!), and as the path starts to descend slightly you'll see the top of the **Old Man of Hoy** ahead. Follow the path to the clifftop, and gaze in awe at this spectacular and famous stack.

The soft Old Red Sandstone stack of the Old Man of Hoy sits on a bed of hard basalt and is 140m (450ft) high. It was first climbed in 1966 by Sir Chris Bonington, Rusty Baille, and Tom Patey. The following year Bonington and Patey returned to be filmed by the BBC for what was the first ever live outside broadcast.

View back to the Old Man of Hoy from the path towards Stours Kinora

3 Keeping a careful distance from the cliff edge, follow the path with the sea to your left. This takes you uphill to a huge cleft in the cliff, known as **Stours Kinora**.

4 From Stours Kinora head directly south across the pathless terrain to regain your outward route in the bouldery moorland, picking up the path back to **Rackwick**. If your visit is in the bird nesting season you will have to retrace your steps back past the Old Man instead.

– To shorten

Do a there-and-back walk to the Old Man of Hoy, which will take around 45min off your overall time.

The Dwarfie Stone

The Dwarfie Stone is well worth a visit, so allow enough time for the taxi driver to stop off there on your way back. It is a huge block of Old Red Sandstone left as a glacial erratic. The stone has been carved out, and is believed to be the only example of a rock-cut Neolithic tomb in Northern Europe, all others being made from piles of rocks. The only similar tombs are to be found around the Mediterranean.

Going down onto the beach at Bay of Sandside

WALK 10

Graemsay: Island circuit

Time 3hr
Distance 10.5km (6½ miles)
Climb 160m

A delightful walk around a rarely visited island, with amazing views

Start/finish	*Graemsay Ferry Terminal*
Locate	*KW16 3NG ///triangle.rave.haven*
Cafes/pubs	*Nothing on the island. Coffee and tea available on the ferry*
Transport	*Ferry from Stromness (also goes to Hoy)*
Parking	*Parking in Stromness at the Northlink Ferry Terminal*
Toilets	*At Graemsay Pier*

This outing is a real away-from-it-all experience, even by Orkney standards! Graemsay is a short ferry journey from Stromness and is a lovely quiet island, with some small but beautiful beaches, expansive views to Mainland and Hoy, and lots of birdlife in the summer. This easy walk initially follows the single-track road, but the rest is on overgrown paths and tracks. The route is signposted throughout.

The Hoy High Lighthouse

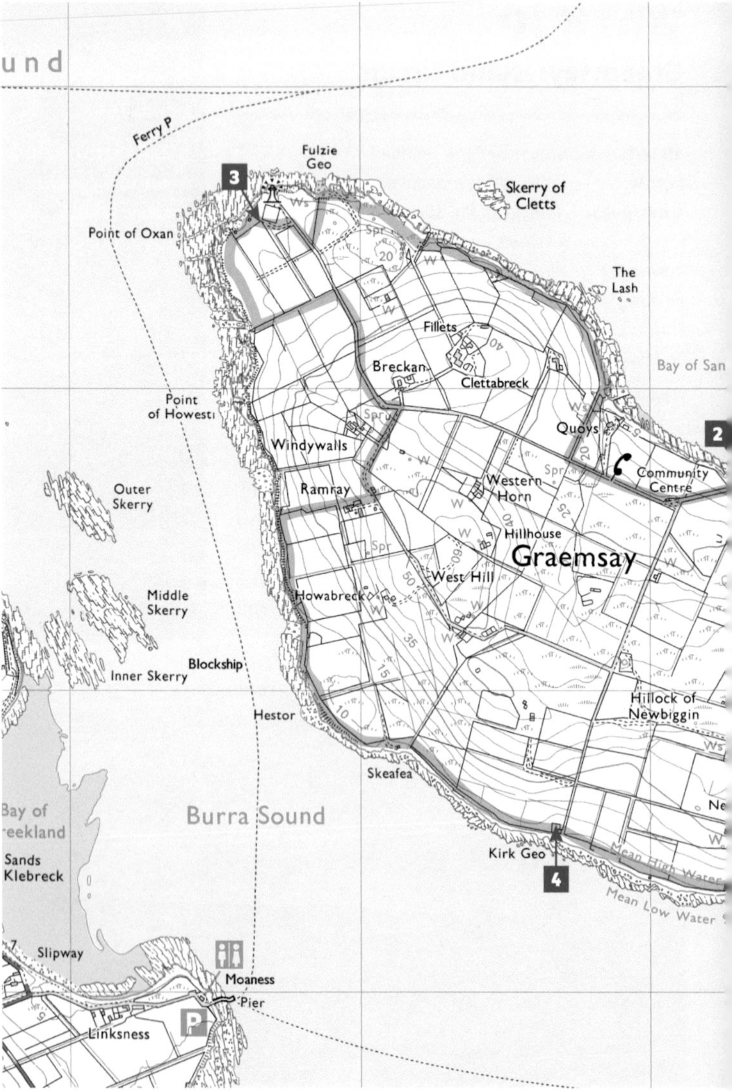
und
Ferry P
Fulzie Geo
3
Skerry of Cletts
Point of Oxan
The Lash
Fillets
Breckan
Clettabreck
Bay of San
Point of Howesti
Quoys
2
Windywalls
Community Centre
Outer Skerry
Ramray
Western Horn
Hillhouse
Graemsay
West Hill
Middle Skerry
Howabreck
Blockship
Inner Skerry
Hillock of Newbiggin
Hestor
Skeafea
Bay of
reekland
Burra Sound
Kirk Geo
4
Mean High Water
Mean Low Water
Sands
Klebreck
Slipway
Moaness
Pier
Linksness

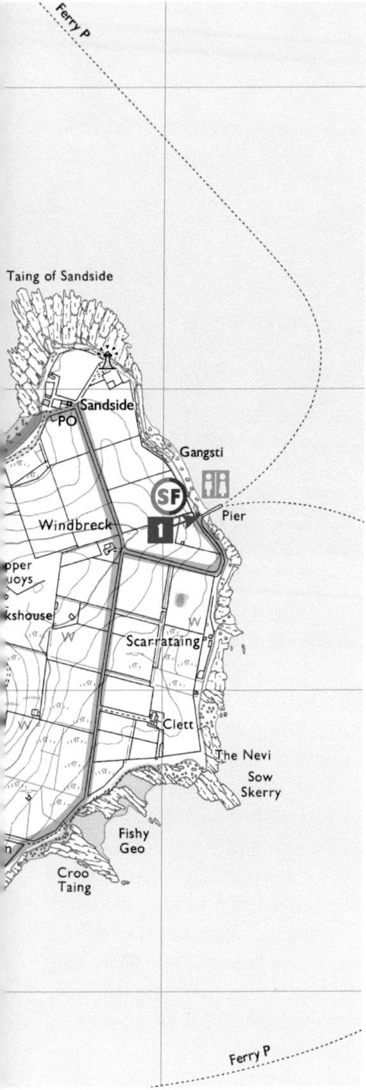

1 From the pier follow the road around a bend to the right, then uphill to a T-junction. Turn right along the road, heading towards the hamlet of **Sandside**. The Hoy High Lighthouse stands on the promontory here. Where the track to the lighthouse goes off to the right, turn left and carry on along the road to the **Bay of Sandside**. Go down wooden steps onto the beach. Walk along the beach with the sea to your right, and at the far end go up a slope to regain the road.

2 Turn right and follow the road past the **community centre** and telephone box to where a green lane on the right leads down to the coast at a Coast Path signpost. Go along the lane, and when you reach the shore turn left, keeping the sea to your right. Follow around the shore, watching for bird nests in the spring and early summer, until another lighthouse comes into view. Go around the back of a pebble beach to a fence, then turn left alongside the fence to reach a track by a gate. Go through the gate and turn right towards **Hoy Low Lighthouse**. As you approach the lighthouse a signposted path on the left takes you down to the shore to reach a pair of gun emplacements.

Hoy Low and High Lighthouses were built in the 1850s by Alan Stevenson. Seafarers entering

The footpath down to the shore, just after the telephone box

Scapa Flow via this western entrance line up the two lighthouses to ensure they have safe passage.

3 Walk around the coast from the gun battery to a stile over a fence. This puts you on a path heading back inland to the track you were on earlier down to the lighthouse. Turn right and walk uphill along the track to a road junction. Turn right along the road, around a left-hand bend to a cottage. Just beyond the cottage a path on the right leads down along the edge of fields back to the shore. Turn left and follow the coast with the sea to your right, all the way to the old chapel and cemetery at **Kirk Geo**.

4 Keep along the coast, with views across to Hoy and into the big natural harbour of Scapa Flow, going down onto the shore then following the path up the low shelf back onto farmland. Go through a gate and across boggy ground via a boardwalk, then back out onto the cliff path, keeping the sea to your right the whole way. Walk around a low rocky headland into **Fishy Geo**, and from here a track goes left, away from the coast. Follow this to the road junction you were at earlier. Turn right and follow the road back to the pier.

– To shorten

Follow the route to Hoy Low Lighthouse and continue to the road junction. Here go straight ahead to follow the road back to the pier. This would give a walk of 8km (2hr).

The sinking of the *Albion*

In 1866 a ship carrying emigrants from Liverpool to New York, and a cargo of pottery, was sunk off the coast near the Hoy Low Lighthouse. The crew had tried to take her into the harbour at Stornoway, but failed, and 12 days after leaving Liverpool the *Albion* was wrecked here, at the Point of Oxan. Most of the people aboard were rescued, but 11 drowned, including a local man named Joseph Mowat who was one of the rescuers. He is buried on Graemsay. Bits of pottery from the ship's cargo are still often found along the shore here.

World War 2 gun emplacements at Hoy Low Lighthouse

View from inside the Mid Howe Broch

WALK 11

Rousay: Mid Howe Cairn and Broch

Time 2hr
Distance 5km (3 miles)
Climb 120m

A short walk to two of the most important archaeological sites on Orkney

Start/finish	*Car park for Mid Howe Cairn and Broch*
Locate	*KW17 2PS ///design.chess.caring*
Cafes/pubs	*At the pier*
Transport	*Ferry to Rousay from Tingwall. No public transport on the island – you will need to take your car or bike*
Parking	*Car park for Mid Howe Cairn and Broch*
Toilets	*At both piers (Tingwall and Rousay) and on the ferry*

This short walk takes in two of the most impressive archaeological sites on Orkney, Mid Howe Chambered Cairn and the Mid Howe Broch. Many people come just for the cairn and broch, but this route also takes you along the shore to the ruined farmstead of Skaill. There are 15 chambered cairns on Rousay, including several just along the roadside on the way to Mid Howe.

Ruined and abandoned farms at Skaill

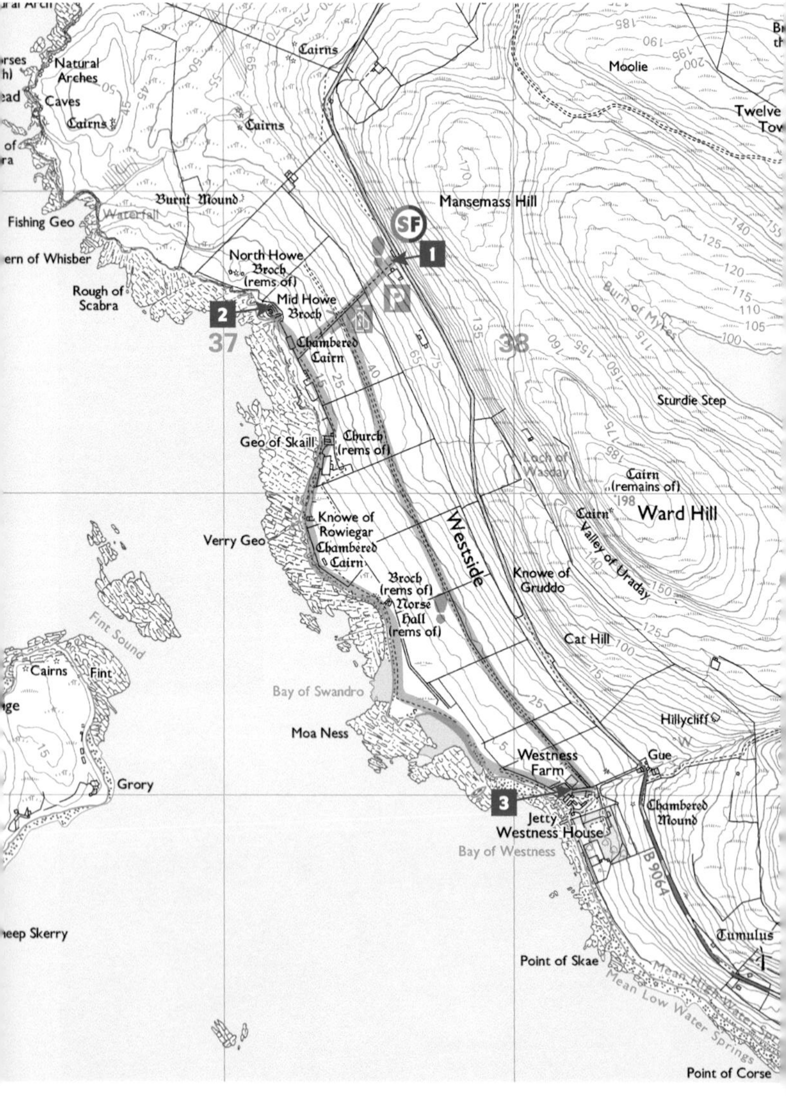
Cairns
Natural Arches
Caves
Cairns
Moolie
Twelve
Burnt Mound
Mansemass Hill
Fishing Geo
Waterfall
SF
1
North Howe Broch (rems of)
Rough of Scabra
Mid Howe Broch
2
37
Chambered Cairn
38
Burn of Myres
Sturdie Step
Geo of Skaill
Church (rems of)
Loch of Wasdays
Cairn (remains of)
Ward Hill
Cairn
Knowe of Rowiegar Chambered Cairn
Verry Geo
Westside
Valley of Uraday
Broch (rems of) Norse Hall (rems of)
Knowe of Gruddo
Fint Sound
Cat Hill
Cairns
Fint
Bay of Swandro
Hillycliff
Moa Ness
Westness Farm
Gue
Grory
3
Chambered Mound
Jetty
Westness House
Bay of Westness
B9064
Sheep Skerry
Tumulus
Point of Skae
Mean High Water Springs
Mean Low Water Springs
Point of Corse

Heading into the Mid Howe Broch

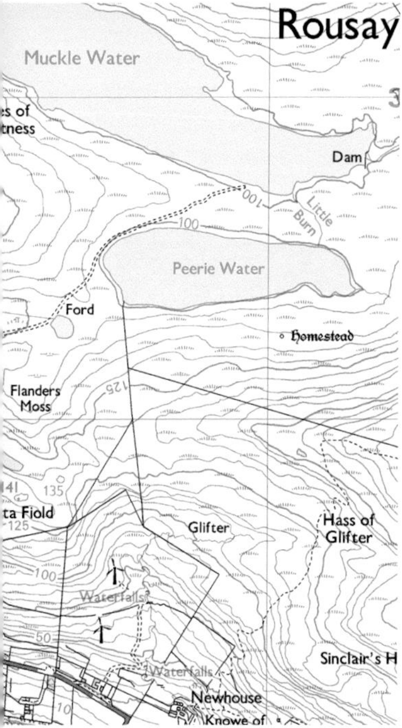

1 From the car park a gate through the fence leads to a path going steeply downhill. Follow this path in a straight line, aiming for the building down at the bottom just above the shoreline. This building covers and protects the **Mid Howe Chambered Cairn**. Go in – it's free, and there are raised walkways inside to allow you to look deep inside the tomb.

Mid Howe is the largest of the 15 Neolithic tombs on the island of Rousay. When it was excavated in the 1930s the remains of more than 20 people were discovered, along with animal bones, worked flint, and pottery.

After viewing the tomb leave the shed at its farthest corner via the exit door. Immediately you'll find yourself looking at the Mid Howe Broch, just on

Returning from Westness on the farm track

the other side of a rocky geo. The Mid Howe Broch is an Iron Age fortified house and would have been at the very centre of a village site.

2 When you've finished marvelling at the broch, walk back past the building housing the cairn (no need to go back inside, as there is a path running along the outside wall). Follow the path until you reach the ruined village of Skaill, where a stile gives access to the beach at **Geo of Skaill**. Continue along the path with the waters of Eynhallow Sound to your right until you reach the farm at **Westness**.

3 As you approach the farm take a track on the left which goes up between the farm and a barn. Walk out along the driveway for a short way, but look for a gate on the left leading to a track. Follow this track back through fields until you reach the path leading steeply back uphill to your car.

– To shorten

Walk down to see the Mid Howe Broch and Cairn, then climb back up to the car park directly. This will take less than 1hr.

+ To lengthen

From Westness carry on along the driveway to the public road at Gue. Go right here over the burn, then left on a track to reach Peerie Water. Return to the road the same way, then turn right to walk along the road back to your car. This will add 3km (1hr) to your walk.

WALK 12

Rousay: Faraclett Head

Time 2hr
Distance 3.5km (2¼ miles)
Climb 100m

A short walk across farmland and moorland to this wonderful headland with views north to Westray

Start/finish	*Faraclett near Banks*
Locate	*KW17 2PR ///remarking.pave.shift*
Cafes/pubs	*Cafe at the pier on Rousay*
Transport	*Ferry to Rousay from Tingwall. No public transport on the island – you will need to take your car or bike*
Parking	*Small parking area at Faraclett*
Toilets	*At the pier*

This is a short but stunning walk through areas of wildflower meadows and heathery moorland where Arctic skuas nest in the summer. The views from the headland are outstanding, especially towards the island of Westray. The walk is on a path through meadows, then moorland, and can be a little difficult to follow, especially on the return leg, but it is worth it for the views alone.

Grass of Parnassus grows on Faraclett Head

Walkers exploring Faraclett Head

1 From the car park walk along the track and where it turns right to the farm at **Faraclett** go straight ahead over a stile. Go up the hill through lovely wildflower meadows full of eyebright, selfheal, buttercups, and daisies and over another stile, then diagonally rightwards, following a path to a gate and signpost. Go through the gate and along the waymarked path as it bends around the flank of the hill. The path keeps well inland from the sea cliffs, and you soon find yourself on the top of the hill where a large cairn sits atop the summit of **Faraclett Head**. From here the views open out to the islands of Westray and along the rugged northern coast of Rousay.

2 From the cairn a path continues along the high ground, with the sea to your right. Follow this across the moorland. The path bends to the left, becoming a bit vague, but soon you come to a kissing gate, then a stile over a wall.

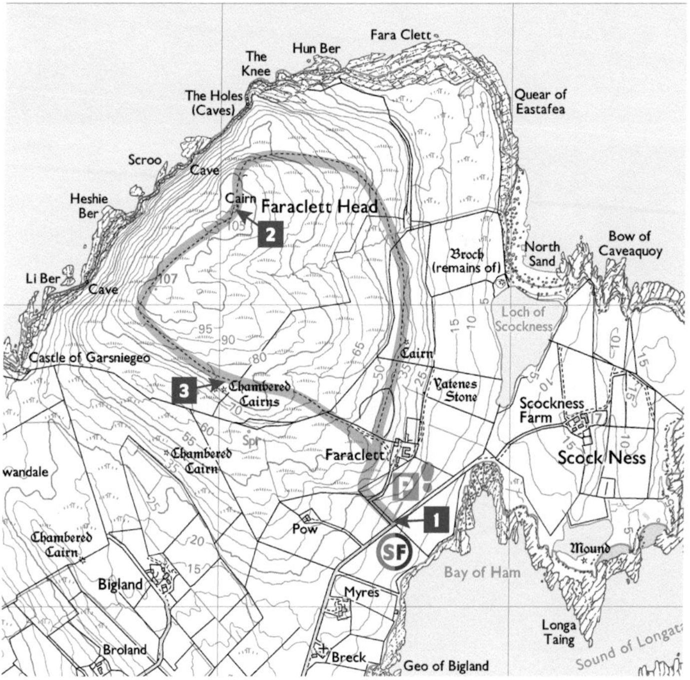

Walkers heading for Faraclett Head

Spring squill, found on maritime heath such as at Faraclett Head

3 Cross the next field, heading in the direction of the farmhouse at Faraclett, and reach another stile. Continue along the path to a farm gate and then drop down the hill to pick up the route you took on the way out. Head down it back to the start.

– To shorten

You could walk to Faraclett Head and back the same way, which is easier to navigate, but not much shorter.

Skuas on Rousay

Great and Arctic Skuas nest on Faraclett Head

Arctic and great skuas both nest on Rousay. Both these large brown seabirds are relatively uncommon, and only nest on remote Scottish islands in the UK. They are great defenders of their nests, and you may find yourself being divebombed if you get too close to eggs or young. The eating habits of both species make them hard to love – they have a habit of chasing other seabirds and forcing them to vomit, thereby providing an easy meal for the skua.

A great skua chick, almost ready to fledge

The start of the path from the Bay of Greentoft towards War Ness

WALK 13
Eday: Ward Hill

Start/finish	*Eday Ferry Terminal*
Locate	*KW17 2AA ///golden.lectured.mermaids*
Cafes/pubs	*None on route. Small cafe on the ferry*
Transport	*Ferry from Kirkwall. No need for transport on the island as the walk starts where the ferry comes in*
Parking	*In Kirkwall*
Toilets	*On the pier on Eday*

Time 3hr
Distance 9km (5½ miles)
Climb 145m

Magnificent views from a hill on the southern tip of this beautiful island

There's always something special about a visit to Eday. Depending on the ferry you catch you may visit Stronsay on the way there, and the crossing is an exciting part of the overall adventure. Once on the island you'll find quiet lanes to walk, stunning coastal cliffs with a few seabird colonies, and an amazing view from Ward Hill, the highest point on Eday.

The Bay of Greentoft

Flaughton Hill
Chapel Hill
Crook
The Old Manse
Newbigging
Zoar
Leeniesdale Hill
Leenies Dale
Stenaquoy Cottage
Stenaquoy
Sch
Burnt Mound
Rowen
Rushacloust
55
56
Backaland
Backaland
B 9063
Roadside
Ward Hill
Groathall
Galtaha
Geo Luon
Neven Point
Costyhead
Cooperha
Whitemaw Bay
Breck
Higha Clett
Sheepfold
Southside
Windyw
Greentoft
Quarry (dis)
Standing Stone
Dyke End
Knoll of Merrigarth
Burnt Mound
Slipway
Mean High Water Springs
Mean Low Water Springs
Bay of Greentoft
The Graand
The Chapel
Clump of Backber
Burnt Mound (rems of)
The Kirk
War Ness
2
3
4
5

1 Walk off the ferry and go along the pier. Ignore the lane to the right and instead go straight ahead, slightly uphill. Turn right at the T-junction and walk along the road to its end at another T-Junction. Ward Hill lies just to the right of straight ahead as you walk along this section of road. Turn left at the T-junction and carry on along the road down to the beach at **Bay of Greentoft**.

2 Turn right as you approach the beach and follow a track along the edge of the beach. Where the track swings uphill to the farm at Greentoft, pick up a path along the grassy bank above the shore. Follow this path with the sea to your left. When it goes into a field keep the fence to your left. The path is obvious and soon takes you to the seaward side of the fence again. Carry on around **War Ness** and begin to climb slightly uphill. Keep close to the clifftops (with care!) for the best views of the cliffs.

War Ness is a good place to see common seals hauled out on the rocks, while the islands of Muckle Green Holm and Little Green Holm host large breeding populations of grey seals. As the cliffs rise beyond War Ness there are small colonies of fulmars, black guillemots, and gulls nesting along this section. If you're lucky you may see a hunting peregrine falcon too.

The low headland of War Ness

The signpost you aim for above the concrete building

Keep going around the coast until you come to the little valley of **Dyke End**. Cross the streams and come to a metal gate.

3 Go through the gate and walk uphill towards a little concrete building. This section is pathless, but the building is a perfect waymarker and

> ⓘ *The Romans came to Orkney in the 1st century* AD. *The Roman geographer Pomponius Mela named the islands the Orcades.*

the going underfoot is just grass. Above the building there is a signpost, and beyond this you'll see the summit of **Ward Hill** at 101m. The summit is marked with a cairn and trig point. The name Ward Hill suggests an early lookout station. There are a number of Ward Hills around the country, not just in Orkney.

4 Leaving the summit keep to the high ground and you'll see a little path going through the short-cropped heather. Follow this and soon come to a track that cuts across the path. Go straight over and after a further 500m come to another track. Turn right and follow the track down to a gate that leads onto a green lane between walls and fences. Walk along the lane to a road junction at the cottage called **Roadside**.

5 At Roadside go straight ahead and follow the tarmac road down to the **Bay of Backland**. The road leads around the bay to the pier.

+ To lengthen

It is possible to continue along the spine of the island to Flaughton Hill by turning left at the first track you meet when heading down off Ward Hill. Follow the track all the way to Flaughton Hill then descend via Chapel Hill back to the road. This adds a further 5km (2hr) of walking.

The summit cairn and trig point on Ward Hill

Noup Head at the height of the nesting season

WALK 14

Westray: Noup Head

Start/finish	*Farm at Backarass near Pierowall*
Locate	*KW17 2DW ///trapdoor.spins.timed*
Cafes/pubs	*Cafe and hotel in Pierowall*
Transport	*Ferry from Kirkwall. Bus from the pier at Rapness to the village of Pierowall 3km from the start (*www.westraybusservice.com*, tel 07789 034289). Ideally take a bike to the island and cycle from the ferry to the start*
Parking	*Very limited parking on the left at Backarass – please do not block access to any gates*
Toilets	*In Pierowall and at the ferry terminal at Rapness*

Time 3hr
Distance 7km (4¼ miles)
Climb 270m

A coastal walk to an important seabird breeding colony on one of the most remote inhabited islands of Orkney

This walk takes advantage of the daily ferry to the remote island of Westray, to explore Noup Cliffs, home to Orkney's largest seabird colony. If you visit in early summer the towering cliffs will be teeming with nesting birds, but it's still a spectacular walk at other times of the year, giving beautiful clifftop views. If you have time at the end of the walk there are some lovely beaches to explore on Westray.

An adult gannet at Noup Head

1 From the farm at **Backarass** walk downhill along the track, then look for a path between two fences that will take you down to the sea. Turn right over a ladder stile and follow the path that clings to the clifftop, with the sea to your left. The coastal scenery here is magnificent, with natural arches as you approach the **Bay of Monivey** then climb uphill around the flanks of North Hill. Just 1km after leaving the Bay of Monivey you'll come to a gate in a fence, with views back down to the sea and **Gentlemen's Cave**.

2 Continue round the coast and a little further on you'll come to the deep cleft of **Ramni Geo**. The path heads inland then around to the other side of the cleft. Below you here is a small gannetry, and during the nesting season you will see these huge seabirds fishing out at sea, diving like darts into the water. The clifftop path beyond Ramni Geo begins to climb and soon brings you to the trig point on the little hilltop known as **Deil Piece**. Take in the views, then walk down the other side of the hill to the lighthouse via a short, awkward rocky step.

The Noup Head lighthouse was constructed in 1898 by David A Stevenson for the Northern Lighthouse Board. In 1964 it was automated, and by 2000 it had been converted to wind and solar power.

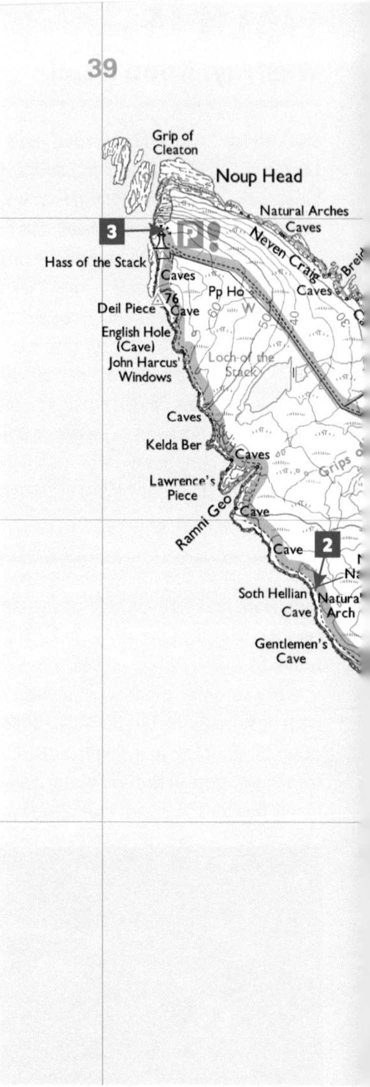

41
42
50
49
Hesti Geo
Point of Scorraber
Bare Geo
Cave
Point of Glemmar
Our Ness
Haa o' Ourness
Kildiver Geo
Knowe of Queen o' Howe Broch
Lean
Sheep Dip
The Lum Head Chambered Cairn
Quarries (dis)
Clemmar
Bay of Noup
Back Breck
Iphs
Farrivald
Mound
North Hill
North House
Noup
4
Skethaquoy
Pierowall
MS
The Hammar
Grip of Monivey
Couters Hill
108
Cairn
Longhouse
Caves
Monivey
Backarass
SF
1
Bis Geos
Lightcost
Ring
Bosan
Natural Arches
Russa Taing
North Bis Geo
Caves
Littlehouse
Hilldavale
Crowals Ber
Waterfall
Natural Arches
Starry Geo
Cave
Natural Arch
MLWS
104

Noup Head lighthouse above spectacular sea cliffs

3 Now walk along the track from the lighthouse, passing Loch of the Stack on your right. Go over a cattle grid, then pass the ruined farmhouse at **North House**. Continue to where the track becomes a tarmac road at **Noup**.

4 Turn right at the sharp bend just beyond Noup and walk along the road back to Backarass.

– To shorten

It is possible to take a car or bike all the way along the track to the lighthouse on Noup Head, and just enjoy a short stroll along the cliffs from there.

Noup Cliffs Nature Reserve

Noup Cliffs is a small but important RSPB Nature Reserve. At only 30m high, and 14 hectares in area, it is surprising that it is home to Orkney's largest seabird colony. The best time to visit is May through to the end of July, when the seabird city is packed with jostling puffins, razorbills, guillemots, and kittiwakes. It can also be a good place to see occasional passing orcas, minke whale, and dolphins, if you are lucky.

The Vat of Kirbuster arch

WALK 15

Stronsay: The Vat of Kirbuster

Time 2hr
Distance 5.5km (3½ miles)
Climb 110m

Stunning coastal scenery and exciting eroded cliffs on a beautiful island

Start/finish	*Kirbuster*
Locate	*KW17 2AG ///tinsel.insurance.documents*
Cafes/pubs	*None on route*
Transport	*Ferry from Kirkwall. On Stronsay you will either need your own car, or there are free e-bikes available (tel Ross on 01857 616339), or a taxi service (tel 01857 616335)*
Parking	*Car park just before the farm at Kirbuster*
Toilets	*No public toilets on route*

This walk around a wild, spectacular headland on Orkney's 'Island of Bays' is one of the best on Orkney for sea views, and as it is rare to find any other walkers exploring here, you get a real feeling of solitude too. The walking is easy for the most part, following a good path, with signposts along the way. Beyond the Vat of Kirbuster the path is less distinct, but just keep the sea to your left until you've reached The Brough and all will be well.

Looking north along the coast from the Vat of Kirbuster

The coast path towards the Vat of Kirbuster

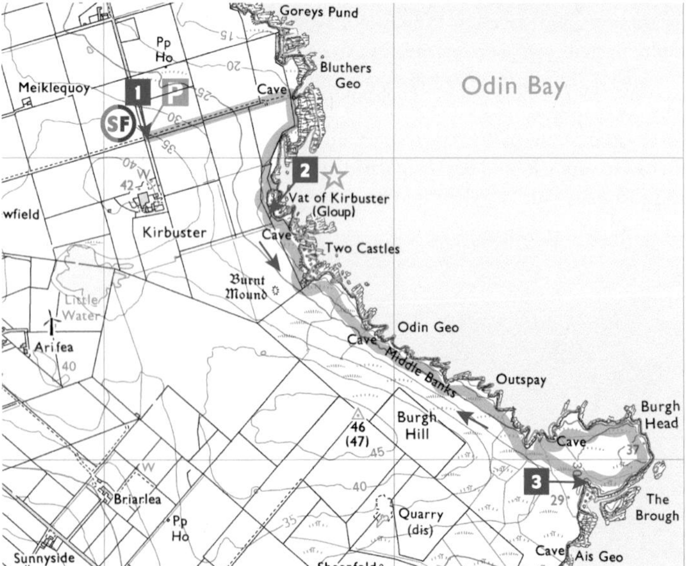

1 From the car park near the farm a gate and path lead down to the sea. Follow this to a gate by a bench and turn right along the coastal path, keeping the sea to your left. Soon come to a rocky inlet and just beyond that a hole in the clifftop with an arch – this is the **Vat of Kirbuster**, known locally as a gloup.

Vat of Kirbuster is a blowhole that has been formed by the collapse of a sea cave. The archway will eventually collapse too, leaving a sea stack. This archway is often said to be the finest in the whole of Orkney.

2 Beyond the Vat of Kirbuster the path becomes less clear underfoot, but it's a very easy walk to follow. Go over a stile and follow the vague path, keeping just above the clifftop throughout. Pass the sea stacks known as **Two Castles**, then beyond them come to **Odin Geo**. The path brings

The cliffs at Odin Geo

The clifftop walk terminates at The Brough

you after 1km to the prominent headland known as Burgh Head. Walk clockwise around the small headland, until you reach a point opposite a detached rocky island full of seabirds. This is **The Brough**. The Brough was once attached to the main island of Stronsay, with an archway leading to its top. It was once the site of a hermitage. A short way further on come to a little valley leading down to the edge of The Brough.

3 From the top of the little valley head inland with your back to the sea, and within a couple of minutes you'll

see the sea again dead ahead. Cross this bit of pathless maritime heath and pick up the coastal path once more. Turn left and retrace your steps via the Vat of Kirbuster to the bench. Turn inland and climb back up along the fenced path to the car park.

– To shorten

Walk to the Vat of Kirbuster and return, without visiting Burgh Head or The Brough – 2km (1hr).

Gannets on their nests at Noup Head (Walk 14)

USEFUL INFORMATION

Tourism

Orkney Tourism
www.orkney.com

Visit Scotland
www.visitscotland.com

Historic Environment Scotland
www.historicenvironment.scot

RSPB
www.rspb.org.uk

Orkney Native Wildlife Project
www.orkneynativewildlife.org.uk

Hoy website
www.hoyorkney.com

Rousay website
www.visitrousay.co.uk

Eday website
www.visiteday.wordpress.com

Stronsay website
www.visitstronsay.com

Graemsay website
www.graemsay.org.uk

Travel

Northlink Ferries
www.northlinkferries.co.uk

Pentland Ferries
www.pentlandferries.co.uk

Orkney Ferries
www.orkneyferries.co.uk

Logan Air
www.loganair.co.uk

Stagecoach Buses
www.stagecoachbus.com

Orkney Car Hire
www.orkneycarhire.co.uk

Hoy: shared taxi service
tel 01856 791315

Westray: bus
www.westraybusservice.com

Stronsay: free e-bikes
tel 01857 616339

Stronsay: taxi service
tel 01857 616335

Accommodation

Orkney Holiday Lets
www.orkneyholidaylets.co.uk

Self-Catering Orkney
www.selfcateringorkney.com

Glossary

broch an Iron Age drystone walled fortified house

brough similar to a broch, but the outer area or wall of a fortified house

geo a rocky inlet on the coast

gloup a sea cave whose roof has collapsed, forming a hole in the ground down to sea level, some way back from the cliff edge. The 'gloup' is the sound the sea makes as it pushed through into the void

ness a headland

ward a hill, usually an old lookout station

wick a bay

First edition 2024
ISBN: 978 1 78631 193 1

Printed in the UK by 4edge Limited using responsibly sourced paper.
A catalogue record for this book is available from the British Library.

CICERONE

Cicerone Press, Juniper House, Murley Moss, Oxenholme Road,
Kendal, Cumbria, LA9 7RL
www.cicerone.co.uk

Updates to this Guide

While every effort is made to ensure the accuracy of guidebooks as they go to print, changes can occur during the lifetime of an edition. Any updates that we know of for this guide will be on the Cicerone website (www.cicerone.co.uk/1193/updates), so please check before planning your trip. We also advise that you check information about transport, accommodation and shops locally. We are always grateful for updates, sent by email to updates@cicerone.co.uk or by post to Cicerone, Juniper House, Murley Moss, Oxenholme Road, Kendal, LA9 7RL.

Register your book: To sign up to receive free updates, special offers and GPX files where available, register your book at www.cicerone.co.uk.